Suits
For
Grooms

Preface

The desire to publish this wedding guide came after I have published the book **Wedding Dresses**. In that book, I gave useful tips on the utilization of a bouquet, veil, head piece and—of course—dresses for brides. It is relevant, therefore, that this book is published to provide useful tips for grooms.

Indeed, the groom is important too. He is the other half of the two that will be joined together in matrimony. He, the groom, is the most important man on the wedding day. Along with the bride, he is the star of the event and the celebrity in front the flashing lens of the cameras.

A wedding is very important, because it is the ceremony which forms the legal union between two people in love. Two people will form this union so that they give themselves to each other exclusively and share and benefit legitimately.

Normally, a wedding is an occasion that requires each invitee to wonderfully dress. It is an occasion for which each guest is to reach into his or her closet for a formal outfit. But notwithstanding all the dressing up and looking good, all eyes will focus on the attires of the bride and groom.

Typically, persons do not pay critical attention to the groom as they do toward the bride. But though the bride takes more of the attention, if the groom fails to make a fashion statement, he will be cruelly criticized.

"A man must look his best on his wedding day," an old man told me. And that old man is very right. Apparently, a man can only be a groom on his wedding day. He cannot be a groom on any other occasion.

It, his wedding, is a special event. What he chooses to wear—as long as it is not a nude wedding—has to be special.

It is not a must that the groom wears a jacket suit on his wedding day. Different grooms have different tastes. Also, different countries have different cultures. In India, grooms typically do not wear jacket suits. Across the continent of Africa, grooms wear robes, beads and skirts, etc. But despite the reality that not all grooms wear jacket suits, and that this book will be read by different people around the world, the book focuses only on suits for grooms.

Whether you will be a groom marrying a woman or another guy, this book is a helpful guide for your upcoming wedding.

Before looking at how to choose and what to wear according to body size and age, here are two independent tips:

Colour matters

There are two particular colours that grooms should avoid. Such colours are green, black, and yellow. A green suit is dull and will most likely not compliment the bride's dress. A black suit will make the groom look like a vampire out of a movie and yellow is too much of a bright colour for the groom.

The colour of the groom's suit should be opposite to that of the best man. It is not fashion-sensible to have a wedding in which the groom and the best man dressed alike. The groom must stand out from every other man on the wedding day. Since the best man will stand next to the groom, the colour of his suit should sharply differ. You do not want to have a wedding in which someone whispers "which is the groom?"

Also, the colour of the groom's outfit must be different from the colour of the bride's dress. If the colour of the bride's dress is white, the colour of the groom's outfit should be of another colour.

The difference in colours between the attires of the bride and groom allows them to each stand out in picture and video.

Don't leave the jacket collar plain; embellish it.

Decorum

The groom should not stand at the altar like a man waiting for a taxicab. He should not stand with folded hands, hands behind him, or his hands moving about his body.

While standing in front the guests and awaiting the entrance of the bride, the groom should stand with his hands clasped in front him below the waist. The same posture applies for the groomsmen.

Suits
For
Paunchy Grooms

When choosing a suit, the groom must not only take into consideration style and colour—but also the shape of his own body. The groom with a paunch should choose a suit that insulates that large and sticking-out belly.

A groom with a paunch looks best in a suit with buttons from top to bottom. A jacket with one or two buttons will allow the paunch to push out and the groom will have to keep adjusting the lower front of the jacket. With a buttoned down jacket, the big belly stays in place.

With a tuxedo suit, the groom's paunch can be held in place to give him a comfortable look, while the jacket plays its part with any amount of button.

Suits
For Young Grooms
(18-40)

Young men are putting some unconventional styles in their wedding suits to portray their youthfulness as well as to represent the fashion of the new generation. It is therefore no surprise when a young groom causes an old man to stare with amazement and—in some cases--shock. But as we all know, the world is not made to stay the same from generation to generation. Things, even for a wedding, change with time. If you are between 18 and age 40, here are suits appropriate for you.

Suits For Older Grooms

(40 and over)

The older groom should choose a suit which gives him a mature look instead of an I-want-to-look-young look. If the groom is age 60 and the bride is age 45, for example, the groom's appearance will not compliment the bride's if he dresses like a 20 years old young man. The more mature, not rather young, the groom makes an attempt to look is the better.

About The Author

Nigel Salmon is a Jamaican author and book writing instructor.